Understanding
the Human Body

Understanding
Reproduction

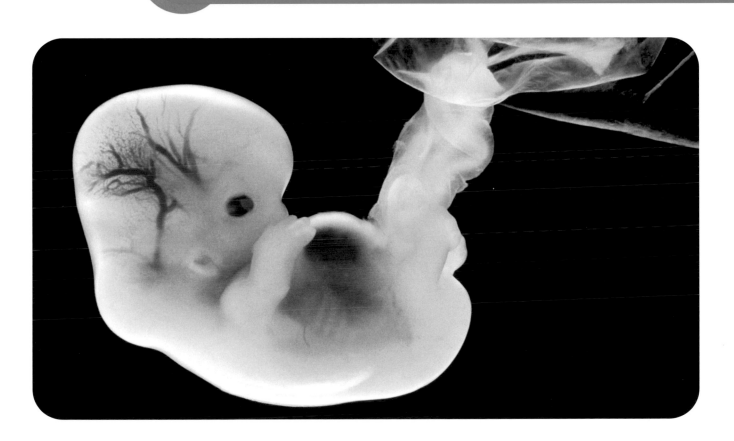

Carol Ballard

rosen publishing's
rosen central

New York

Published in 2010 by The Rosen Publishing Group Inc.
29 East 21st Street, New York, NY 10010

First Edition

Library of Congress Cataloging-in-Publication Data

Ballard, Carol.
 Understanding reproduction / Carol Ballard.
    p. cm. -- (Understanding the human body)
 Includes index.
 ISBN 978-1-4358-9682-6 (library binding)
 ISBN 978-1-4358-9688-8 (paperback)
 ISBN 978-1-4358-9699-4 (6-pack)
 1. Generative organs--Juvenile literature. I. Title.
 QP251.5.B35 2010
 612.6--dc22

                              2009028250

Photo Credits:
Istockphoto.com: cover (Adam Borkowski); p. 10 (Alex Brosa), p. 23 (Sven Hoppe),
p. 31 (Achim Prill), p. 35 (Johnny Scriv), p. 36 (geotrac), p. 37 (Jacqueline Hunkele);
Getty Images: p. 15 (Dr. David Phillips), p. 33 (Neil Harding); Science Photo Library:
p. 17 (Steve Gschmeissner), p. 19 (Steve Gschmeissner), p. 24 (Eye of Science),
p. 27 (JJP/Philippe Plailly/Eurelios), p. 34 (Edelmann); Shutterstock: p. 6 (Monkey
Business Images), p. 7 (Cathy Keifer), p. 9 (Tracy Whiteside), p. 11 (Ilya Rabkin),
p. 21 (Marin), p. 22 (Hanna Mariah), p. 25 (Monkey Business Images), p. 26
(Andresr), p. 29 (Oshchepkov Dmitry), p. 39 (Maxim Tupikov), p. 40
(Tap10), p. 41 (Lev Dolgachov), p. 42 (Monkey Business Images),
p. 43 (Tara Flake).

Manufactured in China
CPSIA Compliance Information: Batch #WAW0102YA: For Further Information contact
Rosen Publishing, New York, New York at 1-800-237-9932

Contents

The life cycle

Reproduction is a basic life process that is common to all living things. It is the process that creates new individuals. Reproduction is essential for the survival of a species, since any species that could not produce new individuals would quickly die out and become extinct.

A process of change

Like every creature, humans undergo a series of changes as they pass through the stages of infancy, childhood, adolescence, adulthood, and old age. You will probably be able to see this in your own family. If you look at photographs of your parents and grandparents at different ages, you will see how their bodies have changed as they have grown older.

The stages of a human life are known as a life cycle. Reproduction is only possible during the stages of adolescence and adulthood.

This photograph shows three generations of a family—grandparents, parents, and children. Each generation is at a different stage in their life cycle.

Infancy and childhood

A newborn baby is small and utterly helpless, depending on its mother or other people for everything it needs. It develops quickly, though, gradually becoming stronger and able to do more and more. During childhood, an individual learns rapidly. By the end of this stage—at about twelve years old—children are able to do most things for themselves.

Adolescence

This is the stage between childhood and adulthood, which takes place during the teenage years. During adolescence, the body reaches its full adult size. Some parts change shape and additional features develop. These are all part of the preparation of the body for reproduction. Although reproduction can occur during the teenage years, most people choose to wait until they are older to start a family.

Adulthood

By the end of the teenage years, most people have finished growing and developing. Their bodies are fully adult and are capable of reproduction. Very little change occurs to the body during adulthood.

Old Age

As people age, parts of their bodies become worn out and may not function as efficiently as before. For instance, many older people have hearing or mobility problems. Illnesses and diseases can also affect parts of the body, for example, arthritis may damage bones and joints. The body gradually becomes frailer, until eventually, vital processes cease functioning and the person dies.

Investigate

There are different life cycle patterns in the animal kingdom. Some creatures give birth to live young, and others lay hard-shelled or soft-shelled eggs on land or in water. Some change little as they grow but others change their form completely. Find out more about the life cycles of different creatures, such as the butterfly, the elephant, the kangaroo, or the crocodile.

The pupa (bottom left), the caterpillar, and the butterfly are just three of the four stages in this insect's life cycle.

Puberty

Puberty is a process that takes place during adolescence. It brings about important physical changes that prepare the body for reproduction. The process of puberty is controlled by chemicals called hormones.

Hormones

The first step in the process of puberty is the release of hormones by a tiny area deep inside the brain called the hypothalamus. These hormones travel in the blood to the nearby pituitary gland, located at the base of the brain.

When the hormones reach the pituitary gland, they trigger the release of two more hormones. These are called follicle stimulating hormone (FSH) and luteinizing hormone (LH).

In boys, FSH and LH stimulate the testicles to produce male sex hormones. The most important of these hormones is called testosterone. In girls, FSH and LH stimulate the ovaries to produce female sex hormones. The most important of these are estrogen and progesterone.

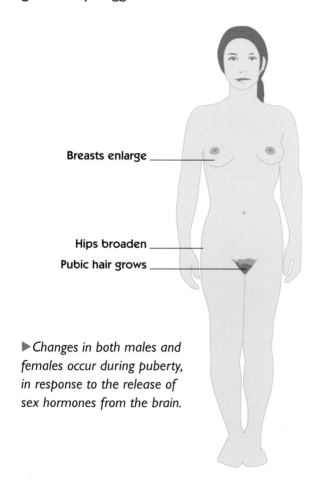

Breasts enlarge

Hips broaden

Pubic hair grows

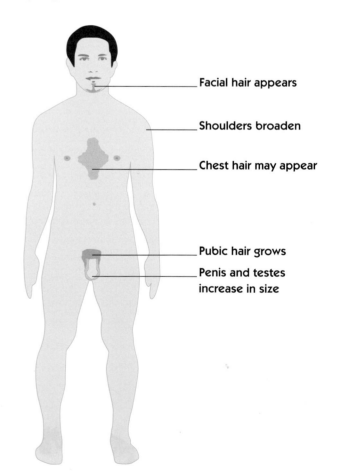

Facial hair appears

Shoulders broaden

Chest hair may appear

Pubic hair grows

Penis and testes increase in size

▶ *Changes in both males and females occur during puberty, in response to the release of sex hormones from the brain.*

As the sex hormones are produced by the sex organs, they are released into the blood and circulate through the body. They help the body to continue to develop and mature, bringing about the physical changes that are associated with puberty. These changes include rapid growth in height, changes in body shape, and the growth of body hair.

Age and puberty

Average ages for the start of puberty are often quoted as 13 years for boys and 11 years for girls. However, puberty can begin at any time between the ages of about 8 and 18, and the changes can take place rapidly or slowly. This means that two people of the same age may be at very different stages in the process. However, neither the age at which puberty begins, nor the rate at which the processes take place affect how an individual develops.

Try this

During puberty, boys and girls do not grow at the same rate—on average, girls reach their adult height at a younger age than boys. If you know your height now, you can estimate your adult height using the chart below:

Age in years	10	12	14	16	18
Boys	1.28	1.19	1.10	1.02	1.00
Girls	1.19	1.10	1.02	1.00	1.00

Find the figure for your age and gender. Multiply your height by the number in the chart. For example, a 12-year-old girl who is 55 inches (140 centimeters) tall would calculate: 55 x 1.10 = 60.5. Her estimated adult height will be 60.5 inches (154 cm).

The process of puberty begins at different ages and continues at different rates in each person.

Body changes

The release of the hormones triggers the changes that take place during puberty. Some of the changes are clearly visible and the person is aware of them. Others take place inside the body and so the person is not aware of them.

Boys and girls

Some changes, such as a sudden increase in height, take place in both boys and girls. Since some parts of the body grow faster than others, young people often feel clumsy and gangly. Other changes that affect boys and girls include the lengthening of the face, the skin becoming oilier, and hair beginning to grow under the arms and around the groin.

Boys

These changes only take place in boys:

• hair begins to grow on the face, gradually developing into a moustache and beard unless the boy shaves regularly

• hair begins to grow elsewhere on the body, particularly the chest

• the voice begins to "break," gradually changing from a child's high voice to the deeper voice of a man

• shoulders broaden and strengthen

• the penis and testes develop and mature, increasing in size

• the testes begin to produce male sex cells, called sperm.

Girls

These changes only take place in girls:

• the development of breasts

• the widening of the pelvic bones, making the hips fuller

Hair has started to grow on this teenage boy's face and so he needs to shave regularly. The hair may be soft at first, but later, becomes stiff and bristly.

Investigate

The skin produces an oily substance called sebum. During puberty, sebum production increases. This can lead to the development of large numbers of pimples, especially on the face. This skin condition is known as acne. Find out more about the causes of acne and how it can be controlled.

- the ovaries develop and mature, increasing in size

- the ovaries begin to produce female sex cells, called ova (or eggs)

- menstruation, often known as "having a period," begins.

Secondary sexual features

Not all the changes that take place during puberty are necessary for reproduction. For example, a man's ability to father a child does not depend on his having a deep voice. A woman's ability to give birth does not depend on her having pubic hair. Their purpose may simply be to make an individual more attractive to the opposite sex.

In the animal world, being physically attractive to the opposite sex would increase the individual's chances of finding a mate. Although human relationships are more complex than this, physical attraction still plays an important part.

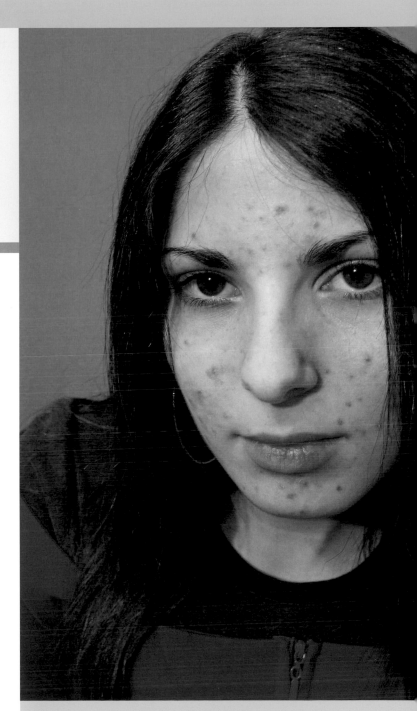

Many teenagers suffer from pimples. Good personal hygiene can help to minimize the problem, but a doctor may prescribe special treatments in severe cases.

Male reproductive system

The male genitals, or genitalia, are the parts of the reproductive system that lie outside the body. They are the testes and penis, which are at the front of the body, between the legs. Other parts of the male reproductive system lie inside the abdomen.

Testes and scrotum Men have two testes, also known as testicles. Each testis is egg-shaped, and contains a network of hundreds of tiny tubes. The testes are held in a loose bag of skin called the scrotum, which is divided into two compartments—one for each testis. To avoid the testes bumping against each other during everyday activities, one usually hangs slightly lower than the other. Because the testes are outside the abdomen, they are 3.5–5.5°F (2–3°C) cooler than the rest of the body.

Epididymides The male body has two epididymides. Each epididymis is a coiled tube that lies around the back of one of the testes. It is linked to ducts from tubes inside the testis.

Vas deferens The male body has two vas deferens. Each vas deferens, also called a sperm duct, is a muscular tube about 16 inches (40 centimeters) long. They form a link between the epididymides and the urethra.

▶ This diagram shows a side view of the structures that make up the male reproductive system. The positions of the bladder and colon are also shown.

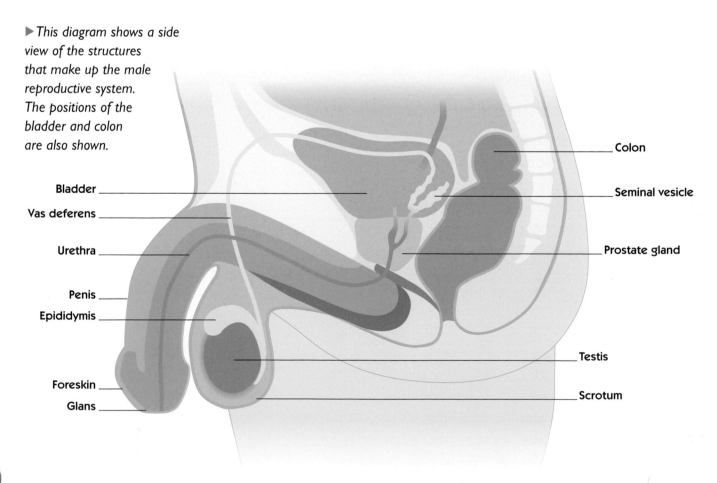

Colon

Bladder

Seminal vesicle

Vas deferens

Urethra

Prostate gland

Penis

Epididymis

Testis

Foreskin

Scrotum

Glans

Seminal vesicles The seminal vesicles are small pouches lying below and behind the bladder. They produce an energy-rich liquid called seminal fluid. Seminal fluid is a major component of semen.

Prostate gland The prostate gland, often simply called the prostate, lies below the bladder and around the urethra. It produces a liquid that mixes with seminal fluid.

Urethra The urethra is a tube about 8 in. (20 cm) long that runs from the bladder to the tip of the penis. The urethra is the route by which both urine and semen leave the body. However, it does not carry both at the same time.

Penis Most of the time, the penis is soft and limp. It contains special tissues that can fill with blood, making the penis hard and stiff. The tip of the penis, called the glans, is very sensitive.

Investigate

Some boys undergo a surgical procedure called circumcision, in which the foreskin covering the tip of the penis is removed. This may be done for religious, cultural, or medical reasons, or simply because it is thought to be more hygienic. Find out more about why people choose to be circumcized and how it is performed.

The glans is covered by a fold of skin called the foreskin. Glands under the foreskin produce smegma, a creamy lubricating fluid that allows the foreskin to slide back over the glans.

In sports where there is a risk of the scrotum receiving a hard knock or blow, sportsmen usually wear protective clothing such as a jockstrap.

Sperm production

The process of sperm production is called spermatogenesis. It begins during puberty and continues throughout a man's life. The process takes place in the testes and epididymides. To produce healthy sperm, it is important that the temperature in the testes remains lower than in the rest of the body.

Making sperm cells

The network of tiny tubes, or tubules, in each testis contains special cells called spermatogonia. These are stem cells, which means they can develop into a new type of cell. Like every human cell except sperm and egg cells, each has a full set of genetic material made up of 23 pairs of chromosomes, a total of 46. When testosterone is released, the spermatogonia are activated.

Cell division

Each cell divides by a process called mitosis to form two new cells. One of these is a new spermatogonium, and it will continue to divide and make more spermatogonia. The other new cell is a primary spermatocyte. This divides by a different process called meiosis, which produces four new cells called spermatids. Each spermatid has a half set of genetic material made up from 23 single chromosomes.

▶ *You can see the structures inside a testis.*

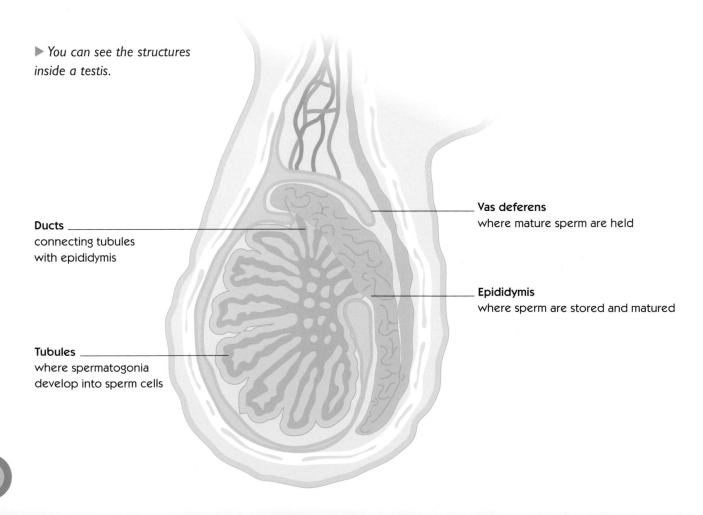

Ducts
connecting tubules
with epididymis

Tubules
where spermatogonia
develop into sperm cells

Vas deferens
where mature sperm are held

Epididymis
where sperm are stored and matured

Body facts

It takes more than two months from the first cell division to the point at which the sperm cell is completely mature.

From puberty onward, the testes contain sperm at every stage of maturation—from spermatogonia, spermatocytes, and spermatids to sperm.

On average, adult men produce more than 100 million sperm cells every day.

Maturing sperm cells

Newly formed spermatids develop into sperm cells. They move from the network of tubes in the testes toward the ducts that lead into the epididymides. The sperm may remain in the epididymides for between 10 and 30 days, until they are fully mature. At the end of this time, they move into the vas deferens and leave the body via the urethra when ejaculation occurs. Any sperm that are not ejaculated break down, and the remains are absorbed by the body.

What are sperm like?

Mature sperm cells are the male sex cells and are also called male gametes. Sperm cells are very small—they are only about 0.002 inches (0.05 millimeters) long and 0.0001 inches (0.003 mm) across at the widest point. Their streamlined shape allows them to swim efficiently.

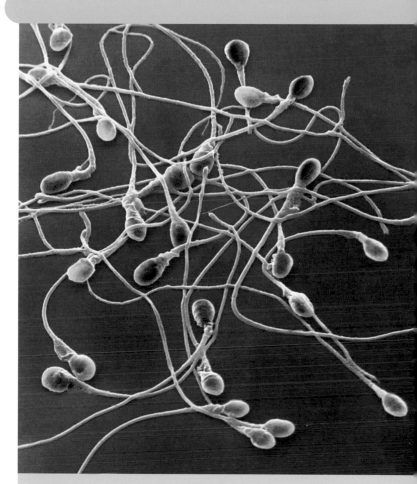

Human sperm cells are tiny. Each has a head containing the nucleus, and a long tail that pushes it along.

Each sperm has two parts—a head and a tail. The head contains the cell nucleus, which contains 23 single chromosomes. The head also contains chemicals called enzymes that can attack cell membranes. The enzymes help the head of the sperm to burrow into an egg cell. The part of the tail nearest to the head contains energy-rich chemicals. These enable the long tail to beat backward and forward, pushing the sperm along.

Female reproductive system

The female genitals, or genitalia, are the parts of the female reproductive system that are outside the body. The major organs lie inside the abdomen, protected by the bony ring called the pelvic girdle.

Female genitals

The female genitals are in the groin between the legs. Although there are several parts, together they are called the vulva. At the front is the mons, a mound of fat that protects the bone beneath it. Pubic hair grows on the skin covering the mons. Between the legs are the outermost parts of the vulva, called the outer labia. These are two thick folds of fatty skin that close over the inner parts of the vulva to protect them.

Beneath the outer labia are two smaller folds called the inner labia. The inner labia meet at the front, covering a sensitive part of the body called the clitoris. Beneath the inner labia are two openings. One is the urinary opening, through which urine leaves the body. The other is the vaginal opening, which leads to the vagina.

The vagina may be obstructed by a thin membrane called the hymen. The hymen usually ruptures and breaks down during puberty.

▶ This diagram shows a side view of the structures that make up the female reproductive system. The position of the bladder and colon are also shown.

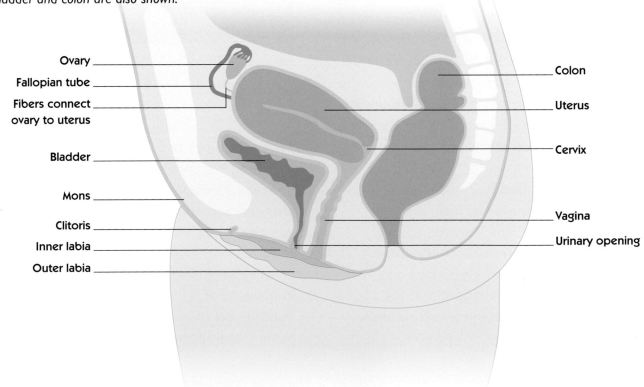

Ovary

Fallopian tube

Fibers connect ovary to uterus

Bladder

Mons

Clitoris

Inner labia

Outer labia

Colon

Uterus

Cervix

Vagina

Urinary opening

These tiny hairs, called cilia, line the fallopian tubes and help to move egg cells along.

Ovaries There are two ovaries, one on each side of the lower abdomen. Each is similar in size and shape to a walnut. Strong fibers anchor the ovaries to the uterus.

Fallopian tubes The fallopian tubes, which are also called the uterine tubes or oviducts, form a hollow, muscular link between the ovaries and the uterus (see below). They are near, but not attached to, the ovaries. Each tube is about 5 inches (12 cm) long. The inside surfaces of the tubes are covered in tiny hairs called cilia. These help to propel mature eggs along the tubes.

Uterus The uterus, which is also called the womb, lies in the center of the lower abdomen. The uterus is similar in size and shape to a pear and has thick, muscular walls. The inner lining of the uterus contains many blood vessels.

Cervix The cervix is a ring of muscle at the lower end of the uterus. It forms a narrow channel between the uterus and vagina.

Vagina The vagina is a muscular tube that is about 4 inches (10 cm) long. Although the walls of the vagina are usually close together, they are very stretchy. This makes it possible for the vagina to expand a lot, for example, as it does during childbirth. The vagina links the uterus to the outside of the body.

Egg production

Egg cells are called ova (one is an ovum) and the process of egg production is called oogenesis. When a baby girl is born, her ovaries already contain hundreds of thousands of immature egg cells. During puberty, these begin to develop and mature, ready for release from the ovaries. The process continues until early middle age, when egg maturation and release stops.

Developing egg cells

Immature egg cells are called primary oocytes. Each one of them has a full set of genetic material made up of 23 pairs of chromosomes, a total of 46. When the pituitary gland releases follicle stimulating hormone (FSH) and luteinizing hormone (LH), the primary oocytes are activated.

Each primary oocyte divides by a process called meiosis to form two new cells. One of these cells is called a secondary oocyte, or ovum. It contains a half set of genetic material made up from 23 single chromosomes. The other cell just contains surplus genetic material. It is of no use and so it simply breaks down and is absorbed by the body.

Maturing egg cells

Each ovum is surrounded by a fluid-filled sac of cells called a follicle. When the ovum is fully mature, the follicle ruptures and releases the ovum. Usually, only a single ovum matures each month. The ovaries alternate, with an ovum maturing in the left ovary one month and in the right ovary the next month.

What are egg cells like?

Mature egg cells are the female sex cells and are also called female gametes.

◄ *Here you can see the structures inside an ovary.*

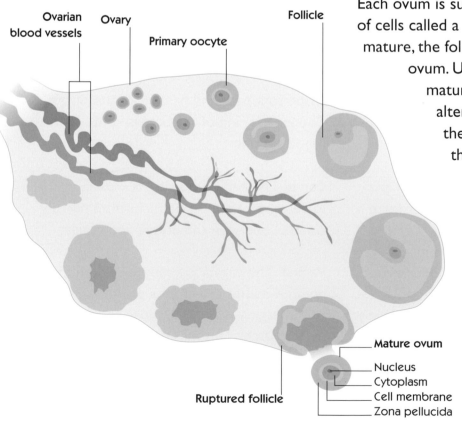

Ovarian blood vessels

Ovary

Primary oocyte

Follicle

Mature ovum

Nucleus

Cytoplasm

Cell membrane

Zona pellucida

Ruptured follicle

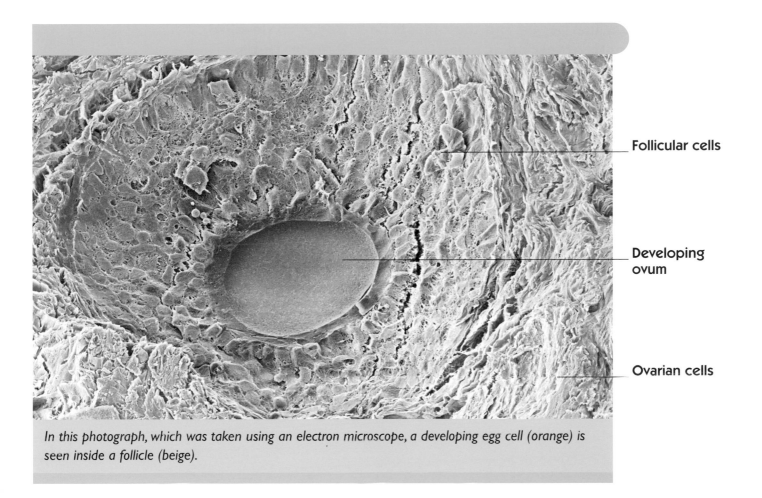

Follicular cells

Developing ovum

Ovarian cells

In this photograph, which was taken using an electron microscope, a developing egg cell (orange) is seen inside a follicle (beige).

Egg cells are much larger than sperm cells. Each egg cell is a round ball that measures about 0.004 inches (0.1 mm) across. In the middle of it is the cell nucleus. The nucleus contains a half set of genetic information made up from 23 single chromosomes.

The nucleus is surrounded by a thick liquid called cytoplasm, which contains nutrients and energy-rich chemicals. This provides everything that the egg cell will need if it begins to develop further. The outer layer of the egg is the cell membrane. This is coated in a jellylike layer called the zona pellucida.

 **Body facts**

Although a baby girl's ovaries contain hundreds of thousands of immature egg cells, most of them break down. This leaves only about 40,000 at puberty.

Only about 400 of these 40,000 egg cells will mature and be released during a woman's lifetime.

The menstrual cycle

Once puberty has begun and the breasts have begun to develop, a regular monthly cycle takes place in a woman's body. This is called the menstrual cycle, from the Latin word *mensis*, which means "month." The cycle is controlled by four hormones: FSH, LH, estrogen, and progesterone.

Length of cycles

In most women, a single menstrual cycle lasts about 28 days from beginning to end. Some women, though, have a regular cycle that is longer or shorter than this, and others experience irregular cycle lengths.

Stages in a menstrual cycle

There are four main stages in each menstrual cycle. The exact timing of each stage may vary from one woman to another, and will depend on the cycle length. The information that follows refers to an average 28-day cycle,

▼**Days 1 to 5** *Menstruation—lining of uterus is shed together with unfertilized egg*

▼**Days 6 to 13** *Uterus lining starts to build up*

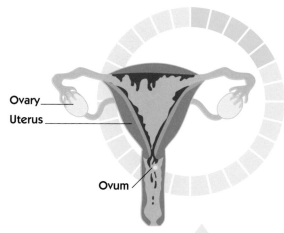

Ovary
Uterus
Ovum

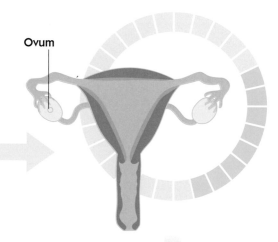

Ovum

▼**Days 21 to 28** *If the ovum is not fertilized, the uterus lining and the ovum begin to break down*

▼**Days 14 to 20** *Ovum is released from ovary*

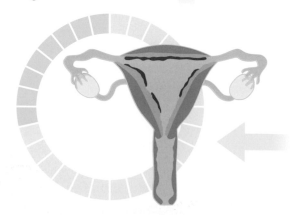

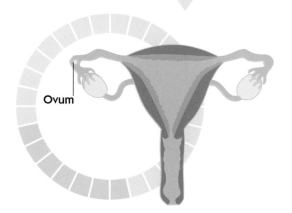

Ovum

during which the woman does not become pregnant. If a pregnancy does begin, the first half of the cycle follows the pattern below, but then a new sequence of events follows.

Day 1: A woman's "period" begins. This is the bleeding from the vagina that occurs in each cycle. It usually lasts between 3 and 5 days. At the same time, the pituitary gland produces FSH, which stimulates one ovum to begin maturing.

Day 5: The bleeding stops. As the ovum matures, the follicle moves toward the surface of the ovary and begins to produce a hormone called estrogen. The estrogen stimulates the lining of the uterus and makes it thicken.

Day 14: The pituitary gland stops producing FSH. Instead, it produces LH, which makes the follicle burst. The ovum leaves the ovary and moves into the fallopian tube. This is called ovulation. The ovum spends several days in the fallopian tube and eventually enters the uterus. The empty follicle, which is now called the corpus luteum or yellow body, begins to produce a hormone called progesterone. The uterus responds to the progesterone by making its lining soft.

Day 21: After having spent a few days in the uterus, the ovum begins to break down. The yellow body also breaks down. Estrogen and progesterone production slows and stops. The thick lining of the uterus begins to break down. On Day 28, which is also Day 1 of the next cycle, the uterus lining leaves the body via the vagina. This is the start of the next period.

Investigate

The hormones that control the menstrual cycle are complex chemicals called steroids. They are transported around the body bound to other chemicals called proteins. Once they reach their destination, the steroids separate from the proteins and are activated. Find out more about these hormones and their structures, and the roles they play during the menstrual cycle.

It is common to feel tired and suffer from abdominal cramps just before and during menstruation. Resting and lying down with a hot water bottle can help to relieve the discomfort.

Sexual intercourse

A pregnancy begins when a sperm cell from a man joins with an ovum from a woman. Sexual intercourse, which is also known as "having sex" or "making love," provides the mechanism by which the sperm and egg are brought close enough to meet and join.

Critical timing

The semen contains millions of sperm that can survive inside a woman's uterus for several days. During most menstrual cycles, a single ripe egg is released at ovulation, about 14 days after the beginning of the last period. It takes an egg one day to travel along the fallopian tubes. Sexual intercourse must therefore take place

People want to be close and to touch and kiss when they are sexually attracted to each other.

within the woman's six fertile days (five days before and one day after ovulation) if sperm and egg are to meet. These are average timings, however, and may vary from person to person.

Contraception

If a couple want to have sexual intercourse without the risk of starting a pregnancy, they may use a form of contraception. There are several different methods of contraception. Some involve using physical barriers to prevent the egg and sperm meeting, some involve taking a mixture of drugs, usually called the Pill, to prevent eggs maturing, and others rely on the regularity of a woman's menstrual cycle.

Investigate

Infections can occur in the reproductive organs and may be passed from one partner to the other during sexual contact. Diseases that spread in this way are known as sexually transmitted diseases (STDs) or sexually transmitted infections (STIs). Find out more about some STDs, such as chlamydia, syphilis, genital herpes, and gonorrhoea. What problems do these diseases cause and how are they treated? Find out which forms of contraception can help prevent the spread of STDs.

Condom

Contraceptive Pill

Using a condom or taking the Pill are common methods of contraception.

When sperm meets egg

After sexual intercourse, millions of sperm may reach an egg in the fallopian tube. However, only a single sperm can join with the egg and begin the process of developing into a new human being.

Race for the egg

When they meet a ripe egg, the sperm cluster around it. The heads of the sperm burrow into the jellylike zona pellucida that coats the egg. This layer contains a substance called ZP3 that acts as a sperm receptor. ZP3 binds to proteins in the membranes of the sperm heads, which triggers the sperm to release enzymes. The enzymes eat into the jelly, allowing the sperm heads to reach the membrane of the egg cell.

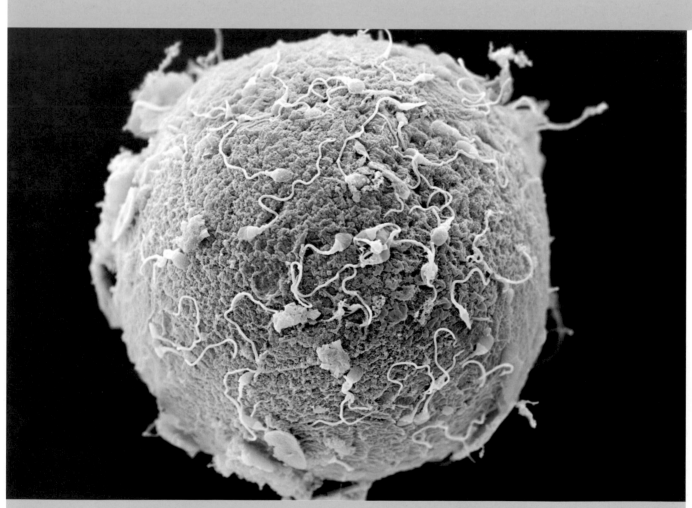

Although many sperm cells (blue) cluster around a mature egg (brown), only one sperm will be able to penetrate and fertilize it.

Investigate

Sometimes a couple have difficulty in starting a pregnancy. In such cases, a procedure called in vitro fertilization, or IVF, may help. Ripe eggs are taken from the woman and mixed with the man's sperm in a laboratory. Resulting embryos can then be put back into the woman's uterus and a normal pregnancy can follow. These embryos are often called "test tube babies." Find out about the history of IVF and the techniques it involves.

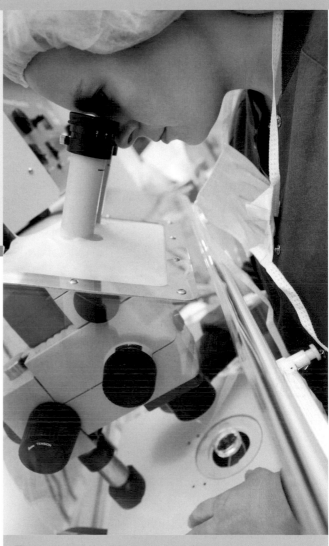

This scientist is adding sperm cells to eggs, an important step in a patient's IVF treatment.

As soon as the first sperm breaks through the egg cell membrane, rapid changes occur in the membrane that prevent any other sperm entering. The zona pellucida (jellylike layer) also hardens, preventing any more sperm from reaching the egg. The penetration of the egg by a single sperm is called fertilization.

Two become one

When the sperm cell is inside the egg cell, the nuclei of the two cells fuse to make a single nucleus. This nucleus contains 23 chromosomes from the sperm and 23 from the egg, making a full set of genetic material with 46 chromosomes. The fertilized egg cell is now called a zygote.

Cell division

The zygote begins to divide to create new cells. The first division begins about 24 hours after fertilization and finishes about six hours later. Each of these two cells divides within one day, to make four cells. Within another day, two more divisions increase the cell number to 16.

As the cells of the zygote continue to divide, it moves slowly along the fallopian tube toward the uterus. More divisions occur, and five days after fertilization, the zygote is a fluid-filled, hollow ball of cells. The scientific name for it at this stage of development is a blastocyst, but it is more commonly called an embryo.

Twins and genetics

The majority of pregnancies produce a single child. However, two or more babies can also arise from a pregnancy. In some cases, the babies are identical but in others, they are not.

Identical twins

The fusion of a single egg cell and sperm cell results in identical twins. At a very early stage in the division process, the developing zygote splits into two separate balls of cells. Each continues to divide, and each develops into a baby. Because they arose from a single fertilized cell, their genetic material is identical. This means that their features will be identical and both will be the same gender. Babies that develop in this way are called identical twins.

Nonidentical twins

The fertilization of two separate egg cells results in nonidentical twins. Two eggs may be released at ovulation and both may be fertilized. Each develops into a separate baby. Because they arose from different egg cells and sperm

Identical twins, such as these sisters, develop from a single fertilized egg.

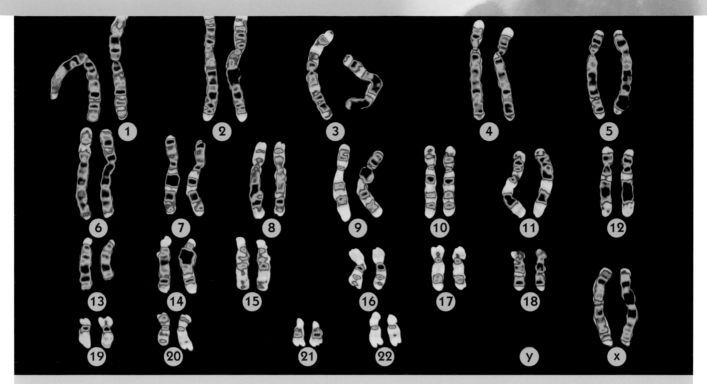

These are the 46 human chromosomes. They are from a female's cells, so there are two X chromosomes and no Y chromosome. A male would have one X chromosome and one Y chromosome.

cells, their genetic material is not identical. This means that the twins will not be identical. They may be of the same or different genders.

Boy or girl?

Each person has a pair of chromosomes called the sex chromosomes. There are two different sex chromosomes, known as X and Y. Girls have two X chromosomes and boys have one X and one Y chromosome. This means that every egg cell contains an X chromosome. But a man's sperm cells have an equal chance of having an X or a Y chromosome.

When the nuclei from egg and sperm fuse, there are two possible outcomes:

X egg + Y sperm = XY embryo = boy
X egg + X sperm = XX embryo = girl.

Inheriting features

Many of your features, such as eye color, are inherited from your parents. They are controlled by small parts of chromosomes called genes. Some genes are dominant and others are recessive. Dominant genes override recessive genes. For example, the gene for brown eyes (B) is dominant and the gene for blue eyes (b) is recessive. A person inherits one eye color gene from each parent. The possible combinations are:

Two dominant genes (BB) = brown eyes
Two recessive genes (bb) = blue eyes
One of each (Bb) = brown eyes (B overrides b)

Other features are inherited in the same way. Some are controlled by many genes, and so the inheritance pattern is much more complicated.

Pregnancy begins

The embryo continues to divide and develop when it reaches the uterus. At this stage, the woman is unlikely to be aware of what is happening inside her body. However, important changes are occurring rapidly. The processes of fertilization and implantation are together known as "conception." When they have taken place successfully, the woman is said to have "conceived" and is clinically pregnant.

Development of the embryo

By six days after fertilization, the blastocyst has become slightly longer and is no longer just a ball of cells. It has an inner mass of cells at one end that will develop into the embryo. Around the outside is a layer of cells that will become part of the embryo's transportation system, bringing nutrients to the embryo and carrying waste away from it.

Implantation

After spending one or two days floating in the uterus, the embryo sheds the zona pellucida (the jellylike layer). The embryo also releases enzymes that help it to attach itself to the lining of the uterus. This process of attaching is called implantation. The embryo's inner cell mass is on the side nearest the uterus wall.

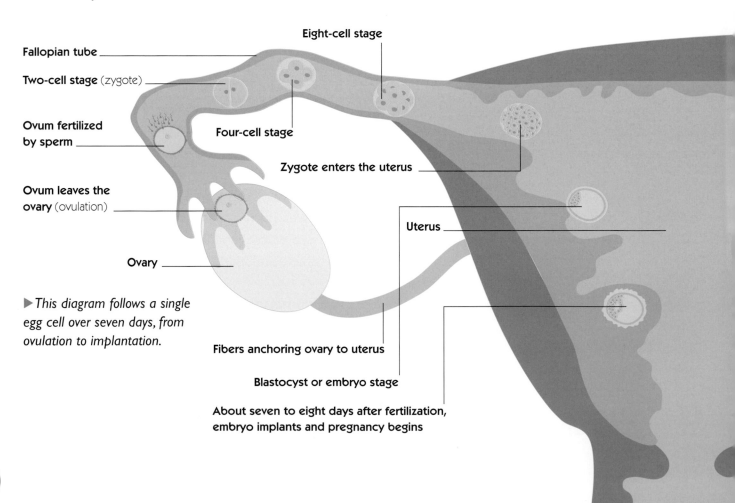

Fallopian tube

Two-cell stage (zygote)

Ovum fertilized by sperm

Ovum leaves the ovary (ovulation)

Ovary

Eight-cell stage

Four-cell stage

Zygote enters the uterus

Uterus

Fibers anchoring ovary to uterus

Blastocyst or embryo stage

▶ This diagram follows a single egg cell over seven days, from ovulation to implantation.

About seven to eight days after fertilization, embryo implants and pregnancy begins

During the next few days, cells of the uterus lining grow around the developing embryo. By about day nine after fertilization, the embryo is completely enclosed by uterus cells. This is the point at which clinical pregnancy is usually considered to begin.

Hormone levels

In a menstrual cycle without fertilization, the levels of estrogen and progesterone begin to fall after ovulation. The presence of a developing embryo in the uterus stops this happening. The embryo begins to produce another hormone, human chorionic gonadotrophin (HCG). This stimulates the corpus luteum to maintain the production of estrogen and progesterone.

Investigate

In humans, most pregnancies proceed with a single fertilized egg leading to a single baby. This is true of some other animals, but in many others, multiple births are common.

Find out about the numbers of young born to a variety of animals. Can you see any links between the size of the animal, the gestation period (the length of the pregnancy), and the number of young born? For instance, an elephant has a gestation period of 645 days, but that of a guinea pig is only 68 days.

Many animals, such as this guinea pig, give birth to several babies in each litter.

Support for the embryo

The eight weeks that follow fertilization are known as the "embryonic period." Following implantation, the embryo and the structures around it change and develop rapidly. From a tiny ball of cells, individual structures begin to develop.

Temporary food supply

The embryo releases enzymes when it becomes implanted in the uterus wall. These break down some blood vessels in the lining of the uterus and blood leaks out of them. The blood contains nutrients that are absorbed by the outer layer of the embryo, providing a temporary source of nutrition for the embryo.

Developing structures

During the third week of development, four membranes begin to form from the outer layer of the embryo. They develop into the embryo's support structures known as the yolk sac, chorion, amnion, and allantois.

Yolk sac

The yolk sac is involved in transporting nutrients to the embryo during the early weeks of pregnancy. It gradually shrinks, and by the sixth week is known as the yolk sac stalk. This eventually becomes part of the umbilical cord, which forms a link between the mother and baby.

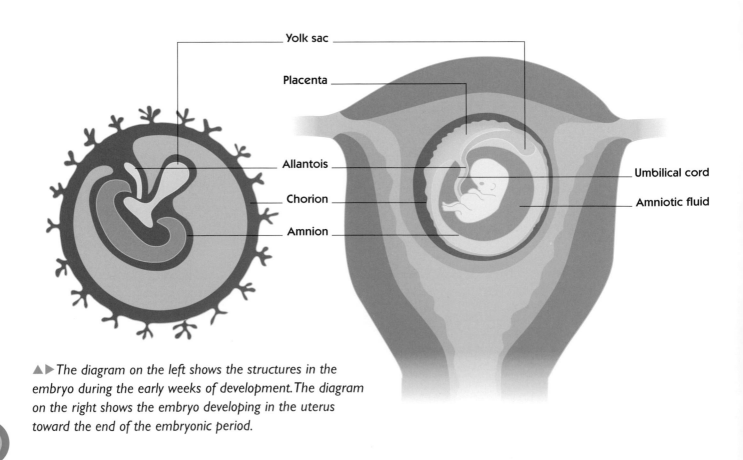

Yolk sac

Placenta

Allantois

Chorion

Amnion

Umbilical cord

Amniotic fluid

▲▶ *The diagram on the left shows the structures in the embryo during the early weeks of development. The diagram on the right shows the embryo developing in the uterus toward the end of the embryonic period.*

Try this

The date when a baby is due to be born can be calculated by counting forward from the date of the mother's last period. Most pregnancies last about 38 weeks from fertilization, so two weeks must be added to account for the time between the last period and ovulation, when the egg was fertilized. This is approximately nine calendar months plus one week. Look at this example:

    Date last period began: February 1st
    Add nine months: November 1st
    Add one week: baby due November 8th

Pick some other dates and imagine they are dates of the mother's last periods. Then try working out birth dates for yourself. To find out when a baby was conceived, you can count backward nine months minus one week from a birthday.

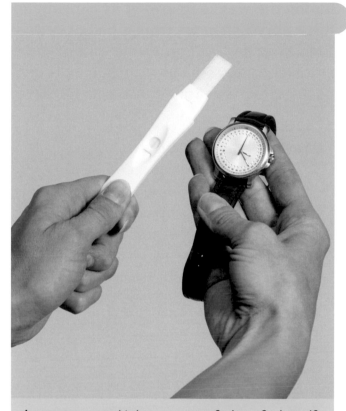

A pregnancy test kit lets a woman find out for herself if she is pregnant. She dips the end of it in her urine and waits for a set time. If she is pregnant, a blue line will appear in the window. If she is not pregnant, there will be no change.

Chorion

The chorion forms a protective layer around the embryo. It contains many fingerlike projections called villi. These allow nutrients, gases, and wastes to pass between mother and embryo. Gradually, the chorion develops into a structure called the placenta, while the rest of the chorion eventually fuses with the amnion.

Amnion

The amnion, or amniotic sac, is a strong, transparent membrane that surrounds and protects the embryo. The space inside the sac is called the amniotic cavity and it is filled with a watery liquid called amniotic fluid. The embryo is able to float freely in the amniotic fluid, cushioned from bumps and jolts.

Allantois

The allantois is a small structure that develops on the wall of the yolk sac. It plays an important part in the development of blood cells. Its blood vessels eventually become the blood vessels of the umbilical cord.

Three to eight weeks

During the weeks following its implantation in the uterus wall, the embryo changes from a ball of cells as its body systems and organs begin to form. By the end of the embryonic period, the embryo contains nearly 1 billion cells and more than 90 percent of the structures found in adults have formed.

Three weeks after fertilization

During this week, development is rapid. By the end of it, the embryo is 0.08–0.1 inches (2–3 mm) long and the head and body can be distinguished. The structures that will become the nervous system, including the brain, begin to develop. The structure that will develop into the heart begins to beat, circulating blood around the embryo.

Four weeks after fertilization

By the end of this week, the embryo is about 0.2 inches (5 mm) long and is C-shaped. The heart develops four chambers and a simple system of blood vessels develops. Tiny swellings that will become the arms and legs appear, and the eyes, nose, and brain begin to form.

Five weeks after fertilization

By the end of this week, the embryo is about 0.3 inches (8 mm) long and has a "tail." The head grows more than the body as the brain develops rapidly. Kidneys and stomach begin to form and major nerves develop. At this stage, any medicines taken by the mother can affect the development of the embryo. Maternal infections, such as rubella (German measles), can also affect the embryo.

Six weeks after fertilization

By the end of this week, the embryo is about 0.5 inches (12 mm) long and the body begins to straighten. Budlike structures appear, which will develop into the arms and legs. Eyes and ears continue to develop and the final shapes of the heart and lungs are established.

Eye beginning to develop

Umbilical cord

Heart

Taillike structure

Leg bud

Arm bud

◀ *Four weeks after fertilization, the heart has begun to develop and leg buds and arm buds are forming.*

Eight weeks after fertilization

By the end of this week, the embryo is about 0.7 inches (17 mm) long and the tail has begun to shrink. Muscles and bones develop and the head is getting bigger to accommodate the rapidly developing brain. The limb buds are growing and hands and feet begin to form. The ovaries or testes are also beginning to form. Now the embryo can make tiny movements, although its mother will not be able to feel them.

Investigate

Medicines and other drugs can affect a baby as it grows and develops inside the uterus. Smoking and alcohol can also affect the baby. Find out more about the ways in which a baby can be harmed if the mother smokes cigarettes or drinks alcohol during pregnancy.

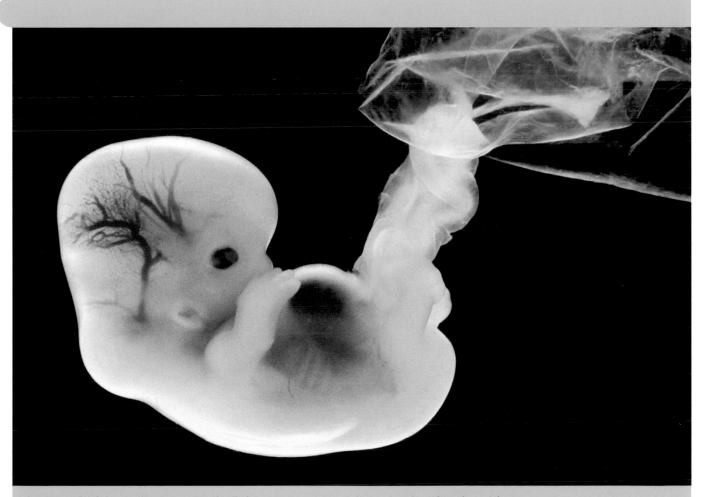

At the end of the embryonic period, all the major structures have developed in the embryo.

Nine to twenty-four weeks

From the beginning of the ninth week after fertilization, the embryo is known as a fetus. The time from the ninth week until birth is known as the fetal period. At the beginning of this time, the main features such as eyes, ears, arms, and legs have formed. The major organ systems have formed and the heart is beating.

9 to 12 weeks

By the end of the twelfth week, the fetus is about 3 inches (7.5 cm) long and weighs about 1 ounce (30 grams). It is recognizably human. It begins to uncurl and its head is held erect, although the head is still large in relation to the size of the rest of the body. The kidneys begin to function and the fetus is able to urinate into the amniotic fluid. The heartbeat can be detected with a stethoscope. Gender differences appear as the fetus begins to develop into a boy or a girl.

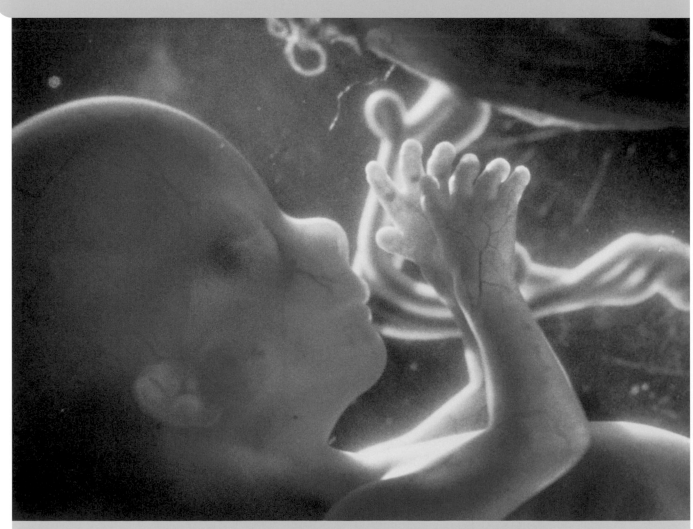

This fetus is between 17 and 18 weeks old. You can see the umbilical cord that links the fetus to the placenta.

Investigate

Tests are sometimes conducted during a pregnancy to find out whether the developing fetus is healthy. There are a variety of tests that can check for abnormalities that indicate the fetus may have problems. Find out about the types of tests, how they are conducted, and what they can show.

13 to 16 weeks

By the end of the sixteenth week, the fetus is about 7 inches (18 cm) long and weighs about 3–4 oz. (90–110 g). The mother is aware that her uterus is swelling. The gender of the fetus is now apparent as the external genitals form. The lungs and brain develop their final shapes. Bones develop further and bone marrow begins to produce blood cells. The mother, who may have been feeling sick during the early weeks of pregnancy, now usually begins to feel much better.

17 to 20 weeks

By the end of the twentieth week, the fetus is about 10–12 in. (25–30 cm) long and weighs about 7–16 oz. (200–450 g). The uterus is completely filled with the fetus, placenta, and amniotic fluid. From now on, the uterus must stretch as the fetus grows. The fetus' body grows more quickly than the head, bringing them more into proportion. Hair appears on the head and fine hair called lanugo covers the body. The fetus is able to stretch and kick, and the mother can feel its movements.

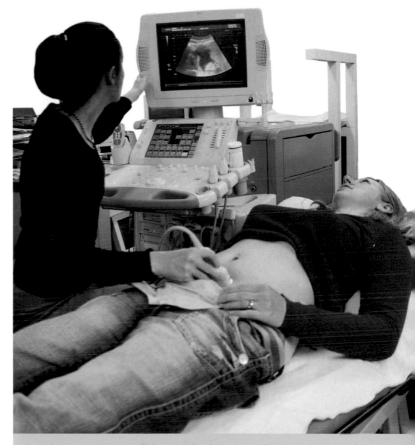

An ultrasound scan of the mother's uterus shows images of the fetus on the screen. Medical staff can check that the baby is developing normally—and the mother can have a photograph of her baby before it is born!

21 to 24 weeks

By the end of the twenty-fourth week, the fetus is about 11–14 inches (27–35 cm) long and weighs about 35–48 ounces (1,000–1,350 g). Its body proportions continue to alter as the body grows more rapidly than the head. The fetus has periods of being awake and asleep, and it is thought that the fetus can hear external noises such as voices and music.

The last three months

As the pregnancy enters the last three months, the fetus is almost fully developed. If it were to be born from now on, it would have a very good chance of survival. Babies born more than three weeks before their due date are said to be premature. The earlier the stage at which they are born, the more medical care they will need.

Final changes

During the last few weeks in the uterus, the fetus develops still further. Its eyelids open and eyebrows and eyelashes appear.

The nervous system continues to develop and the brain gets bigger. The fetus may begin to suck its thumb. It begins to accumulate fat, so its weight increases and its skin becomes less wrinkly.

In late pregnancy, the fetus also loses the lanugo (body hair) that covered it. Its nails grow long and reach the ends of the fingers and toes. In a male fetus, the scrotum develops and the testes slowly descend into it.

Although most of the fetus' internal organs are fully formed and in their final positions, its lungs are still developing. The lungs do not begin to function until after birth.

Using a stethoscope, this doctor can check that the baby's heart is beating normally.

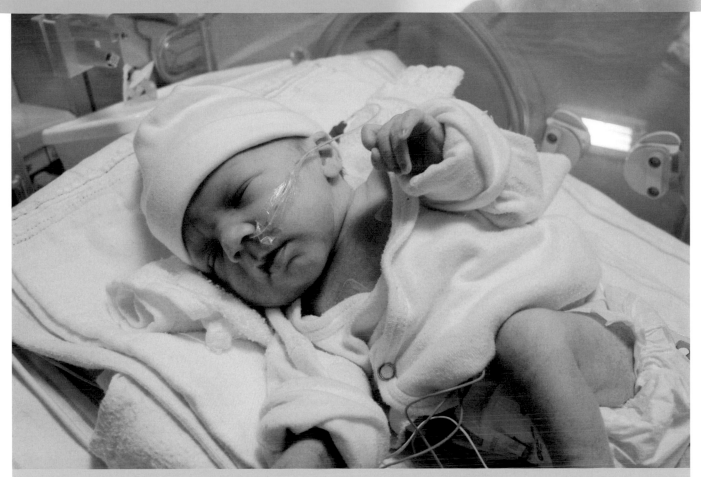

A premature baby may need to spend some time in an incubator after it is born. This can help the baby to breathe, and hospital staff can monitor its health.

Getting into position

About four weeks before it is due to be born, the fetus turns around in the uterus. It usually positions itself head-down, although sometimes a fetus takes the opposite position with its feet downward. This is called a "breech position," and it can make the birth difficult. The fetus cannot turn around again, because it fills the uterus that has reached the limit of its stretchiness. Its movements are now restricted.

From its head-down position, the fetus's head drops down into the space surrounded by the mother's pelvis, ready for birth.

Investigate

Premature babies need specialist medical care. They are smaller and lighter than babies born after a full-length pregnancy. Some of their organs, particularly their lungs, are likely to be underdeveloped. They usually need to spend time in an incubator, which can assist the baby with its breathing. Find out more about the needs of premature babies and how they are cared for.

Childbirth

The process of birth is called labor, or childbirth, and it has three stages. The length of time that labor takes varies greatly. Most births take about 12 hours, although many are much shorter or longer than this.

First stage

Some women become aware that labor is starting when they feel cramplike pains in their abdomen. These pains occur when the muscles of the uterus contract, and they are called contractions. For others, the first sign that labor is about to begin is fluid flowing out of the vagina. This is the amniotic fluid, which rushes out when the amnion ruptures.

The contractions of the uterus gradually pull on the cervix and make it wider. The baby's head presses on the cervix, and this pressure also helps to make the cervix open wider.

Normally, the opening of the cervix is about 0.08 inches (2 mm) wide, but it has to open to about 4 inches (10 cm) to allow the baby's head to pass through.

▼ *These diagrams show the three stages of labor.*

Cervix begins to widen

Uterus contracts

Umbilical cord

Vagina

▲ *Stage 1: The baby is inside the uterus with its head against the cervix. The cervix is slightly widened.*

Umbilical cord

Placenta breaks away from uterus wall

Amnion

▲ *Stage 3: The umbilical cord is attached to the placenta. The umbilical cord is partially outside the body and the placenta is pulling away from the uterus.*

Cervix is fully open

Baby is pushed out of mother's body

Vagina

▲ *Stage 2: The cervix is open and the baby's head is emerging through the birth canal.*

The first stage of labor is the longest and can take several hours. Initially, a contraction is felt every 20 to 30 minutes. As labor progresses, the contractions become more frequent until, by the time the cervix is fully open, they occur about every two minutes.

Second stage

With the cervix fully open, the baby's head can move into the vagina. The walls of the vagina are very stretchy so the baby can pass through it. As the uterus continues to contract, the baby is pushed out of the mother's body. The baby can begin to breathe as soon as its head and chest have left the mother's body.

Third stage

Although the baby has left its mother's body, they are still linked by the umbilical cord. A medical worker such as a doctor, nurse, or midwife will clamp the umbilical cord in two places and then cut it between the clamps. Soon after the baby has been born, the placenta breaks away from the uterus wall. It leaves the mother's body through the vagina, along with the empty amnion and the umbilical cord. Together, these parts are called the afterbirth.

Cesarean birth

Sometimes, doctors know in advance that for some reason a normal labor will not be possible. In other cases, labor may begin normally but problems arise during the birth. In such cases, doctors can perform a procedure called a cesarean. They cut through the mother's abdomen and uterus and lift the baby and placenta out.

Newborn baby

A newborn baby needs a lot of care and attention. Medical staff check it to see that it has no health problems. They then weigh it and measure it. The baby may be nourished with milk from the mother's breast. If the mother is unable to produce milk for her baby, it may be fed a special milklike liquid from a bottle.

A newborn baby may seem to be doing little more than the basic life processes of breathing, eating, and getting rid of waste. Most sleep for many hours every day. However, during its waking periods, the most active areas of a newborn's brain are those involved with processing sights, sounds, smells, tastes, and touch, as the sense organs collect information about the baby's surroundings.

Feeding her newborn baby can be an intimate experience and help mother and baby to form a strong bond.

Fun facts

This young kangaroo finishes developing in its mother's pouch.

Making history
The first "test tube baby" was born on July 25, 1978. She was a girl named Louise Brown. Louise Brown celebrated her 21st birthday in 1999, by which time 300,000 women worldwide had conceived through IVF.

The longest...
At 645 days, the Asian elephant has a longer gestation period than any other animal.

...and the shortest
Domestic white mice have a gestation period of 12–13 days, the shortest known among nonmarsupial mammals.

Growing pouch
Marsupials, such as kangaroos and opossums, give birth before their young are fully developed. The young then stay in the mother's pouch to complete their development.

Sex change
Oysters can change gender. Most start life as males and turn into females as they grow older.

Two in one
Worms are hermaphrodites, which means each individual has both male and female sex organs and produces both eggs and sperm. They need to mate to reproduce, though, since an individual's sperm cannot fertilize its own eggs.

First responses
A newborn baby responds instinctively to some situations. These responses are called reflexes. For example, if a baby is laid on its back and its head is turned to one side, it will extend its arm and leg on that side and bend the opposite arm and leg.

Deadly attraction
Female Black Widow spiders sometimes kill and eat their mates after mating.

Death follows birth
Salmon migrate from the sea to fresh water to mate. In some salmon species, such as the Chinook, the female lives for just a few days after laying her eggs.

Changing form
Insects, amphibians, and some other types of animal change their form one or more times during their life cycle.

Dolly the sheep

Cloning is a process of creating a new individual from the cells of one individual. The first animal to be successfully cloned was a sheep named Dolly. She was created in 1996 by scientists in Edinburgh, Scotland.

Milk protection

As well as nutrients, a mothers' milk contains chemicals called antibodies that help to protect her baby against infections and other diseases.

Mini-teeth

Although a newborn baby has no teeth, they are all perfectly formed inside the gums, ready to penetrate the gums when the baby is about 4 months old.

Sleepyheads

Most babies sleep for 14–18 hours every day for the first three months after birth.

Taking a break

Most women gain 20–29 pounds (9–13 kg) during pregnancy. Of this, only about 7 pounds (3 kg) is the weight of the baby—the rest is due to changes such as enlargement of the breasts, presence of amniotic fluid, development of the placenta, and storage of some fat.

Early births

Over 500,000 babies are born prematurely in the United States every year. The youngest surviving premature baby was a boy named James Elgin Gill, born on May 20, 1987, in Ottawa, Canada, after a pregnancy that lasted just 21 weeks and 5 days. He weighed only

Only a small part of the weight a mother puts on during pregnancy is the weight of the baby.

22 oz. (624 g), but survived and developed into a normal, healthy child.

Fossilized eggs

Dinosaurs hatched from hard-shelled eggs similar to those of reptiles and birds. The biggest fossilized dinosaur eggs were found in France and were 12 in. (30 cm) long and 10 in. (25 cm) wide, with a volume of about 4.2 pints (2 liters). The smallest fossilized dinosaur eggs were less than 1.8 in. (3 cm) long and were found in South America.

Activities

Blue or brown?

Use these diagrams of eye color inheritance to work out what color eyes each child will have:

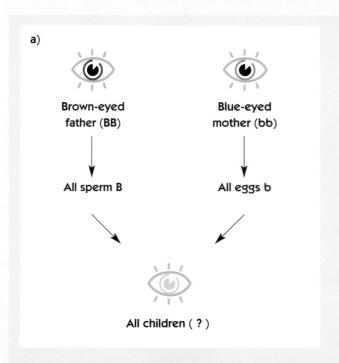

a)

Brown-eyed
father (BB)

Blue-eyed
mother (bb)

All sperm B

All eggs b

All children (?)

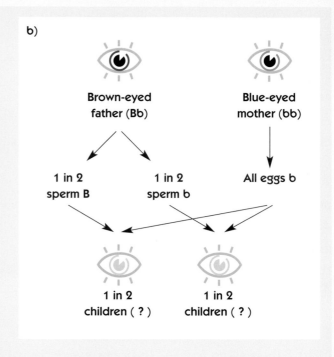

b)

Brown-eyed
father (Bb)

Blue-eyed
mother (bb)

1 in 2
sperm B

1 in 2
sperm b

All eggs b

1 in 2
children (?)

1 in 2
children (?)

A person inherits one eye color gene from each parent, but children born to the same parents do not always share the same eye color. This happens because they have inherited a different combination of eye color genes.

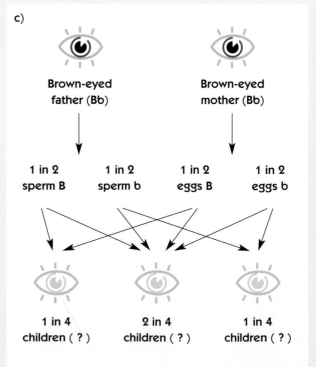

c)

Brown-eyed
father (Bb)

Brown-eyed
mother (Bb)

1 in 2
sperm B

1 in 2
sperm b

1 in 2
eggs B

1 in 2
eggs b

1 in 4
children (?)

2 in 4
children (?)

1 in 4
children (?)

Fertilization of a human egg takes place about 2 weeks after the mother's period. The baby that then develops is normally born about 38 weeks after fertilization.

Calculating birth dates

On page 31, you read about how to calculate the date a baby is due to be born. Using that information, now try to figure out when a baby would be due if the mother's last period started on:

a) May 11

b) July 7

c) September 24

d) November 30

e) December 27

f) March 7

Sequence of events

Put these events into the order in which they occur during pregnancy:

a) fetal hair appears

b) backbone and brain begin to develop

c) mother misses period

d) fetal heart beat can be heard

e) fertilization of egg by sperm

f) fetal head drops into mother's pelvis

g) fetus about 13 inches (33 cm) long

Glossary

adolescence the stage between childhood and adulthood

amnion (amniotic sac) the membrane that encloses the fetus and amniotic fluid

amniotic fluid the liquid that surrounds the fetus in the uterus

blastocyst a ball of cells, also called the embryo

cervix the lower end of the uterus

chromosome one of the structures that carries genetic information

conception the beginning of a pregnancy

corpus luteum the empty follicle left from a ripe egg cell

ejaculation the movement of semen into the vagina

embryo the developing baby in the early weeks of pregnancy

enzyme a chemical that assists in a chemical reaction

epididymis the coiled tube around the back of a testis

fallopian tube the tube that links an ovary with the uterus

fertilization fusion of a sperm cell and an egg cell

fetus the developing baby after the ninth week of pregnancy

gamete an egg or sperm cell

hormone a chemical produced by the body that controls various processes

implantation the embedding of the embryo in the uterus wall

labor the process of birth

meiosis the division of a cell to produce four new cells

menstruation the monthly loss of blood and uterus lining, also called a period

mitosis the division of a cell to produce two new cells

oocyte an immature egg cell

oogenesis the process of egg production and maturation

ovary the organ in which egg cells mature

ovum the female gamete

penis the male sex organ

placenta the structure through which a fetus receives nutrients and gets rid of wastes

prostate the gland that lies below the bladder in males

puberty the sequence of changes that occur during adolescence

scrotum the sac that holds the testes

semen fluid that contains sperm

seminal fluid energy-rich liquid that forms part of the semen

sperm male gamete

spermatid an immature sperm cell

spermatocyte cell from which four spermatids are formed

spermatogenesis the process of sperm production

testes the organs where sperm are produced

umbilical cord the cord that links fetus and placenta

urethra the tube through which semen and urine leave the body in males; in females, only urine travels through the urethra

vagina the tube leading from the uterus to the outside of the body

vas deferens the tube that links the epididymis and the urethra

vulva the external female genital organs

zygote a fertilized egg cell

Further Information and Web Sites

Exploring The Human Body: Reproduction And Growth by Michaela Miller (KidHaven Press, 2005)

Human Reproduction And Development by A Cassan (Chelsea Clubhouse, 2005)

What Happens When You Are Born And Grow? by Jacqui Bailey (PowerKids Press, 2008)

Web Sites
Due to the changing nature of Internet links, Rosen Publishing has developed an online list of Web Sites related to the subject of this book. This site is regularly updated. Please use this link to access this list: http://www.rosenlinks.com/uhb/repr

Index